THE
H
MYSTERY

BETTE PAUL

LDA

The Doone House Mystery
00693E
ISBN 1 85503 154 X

First published 1992
Reprinted 1993, 1995, 1997

LDA, Duke Street, Wisbech, Cambs, PE13 2AE

1

Nell's Bikes

'Hey, look, at that!' Dan pointed across the village street to a tall, dark girl. The girl was putting bikes out by the corner shop. 'She's a bit of all right, isn't she? And the bikes look OK too,' he added.

Pete didn't look up from the stone he was kicking. 'So what?' he asked in a dull voice. He kicked the stone and watched it shoot along the gutter. 'We can't just go and buy a bike,' he said.

'No, but we can go and chat up the girl at the shop.' Dan grinned and set off across the road. 'Come on, let's get some fun out of our free day.'

'Fun? In this place? You'll be lucky.' Pete kicked his stone down the street and slowly followed Dan. The two of them had come to Devon on a training course. They'd been on a twenty-mile walk, climbed down some caves and learned how to paddle a canoe. They'd enjoyed all that, though

Pete didn't see how paddling a canoe was going to get him a job back home in the town. Now they had a free day and it looked like being a total flop. The village had only one street, two shops and a pub and even Dan couldn't make them exciting.

When Pete reached the shop Dan was reading a notice by the side of the bikes and counting his money. There was no sign of the girl.

'Look, Pete, we can hire bikes. Have you got any money?'

Pete glanced quickly at the notice where all the prices were shown. 'Yeah,' he said. 'I've got a lot more than £1.50.'

'That's just for an hour, you great nerd!' Dan said. 'Look at it carefully, Pete – it's £5 for the day.' Dan pointed at the price.

Pete pushed his hand through his blond, cropped hair. 'Oh yeah, you're right,' he said. He wasn't surprised, he was always making mistakes and Dan was always putting him right.

'I'm right about the girl, too,' Dan grinned. 'Come on, we've got an excuse to chat her up, now.'

But Pete was counting his money and checking the notice. 'Hang about,' he said. 'It says something here about a deposit.'

Dan peered at the list. 'Oh, hell, and it's £10 per cycle. Have you got that much?'

Pete shook his head. The training course was free but he'd only got last week's giro for spends. He looked at the two mountain bikes and opened his eyes wide. 'Wow!' he said. 'Just look at these!' They were the best bikes Pete had ever seen; he was dying to ride one. But they still hadn't got a deposit.

Dan sighed. 'I was hoping we'd found something to do. I wish we'd gone walking over the moors with the others now.'

'Hang on a minute!' Pete had just seen something else on the notice. 'What's the name of the place where we're staying?' he asked.

'Doone Hall, of course, you great nit! Can't you remember anything?'

'Well then, Professor Brainbox, just look at that!' Pete pointed to the bottom of the board and read, slowly and clearly. '"No deposit terms for the residents of Doone Hall Youth Hostel."'

'Hey – yeah – you're right!' Dan read the words. 'Great, we only need £5 each for the day. Come on!'

The bell on the shop door pinged as they went in. The shop was so quiet that even the bikes propped up round the walls seemed to be sleeping. They were waiting to be mended or cleaned and didn't look fit to be hired out.

Dan nudged Pete. 'They look a bit done for,' he said. 'I hope we don't have to take one of those.'

'I think that one's dead,' said Pete, pointing to a bike that was tipped on its seat with its wheels in the air.

'Poor old thing,' Dan grinned and pushed the pedals so that the wheels spun round. 'Come along now, old dear, Danny will soon get you going!'

'Steady on, it needs some oil. You'll have the chain off in a minute.' Pete loved bikes. He couldn't bear to see Danny mess about with this one. He bent over the wheels to stop them turning and didn't see the tall girl come from the back of the shop.

'Good morning,' she said. 'Can I help you?'

The two boys turned to look at her. She wore denim overalls and a bright, checked shirt, which showed smooth tanned skin at the neck. She looked at the boys with clear, blue eyes – then she saw the wheels spinning round and smiled and shook her head, as if she knew they'd been messing about.

Dan looked up at her and put on his best smile. 'We'd like two bikes, please.'

'For the day, or the week?' she asked, looking across at Pete.

'Er...' said Pete, looking down at her feet. 'Er...' he said again, and blushed. He looked at Dan. Dan looked at him. Pete never had much to say even to his mates, and he was hopeless with girls; he never knew how to talk to them.

The tall girl smiled at Pete. 'Was it just for the day, then?' she asked in her soft, Devon voice.

'That's right, just for the day,' Dan cut in. He looked all round. 'But we need good ones.'

'Well, I'm still working on these,' said the girl. 'But there are two good mountain bikes outside. You can try them.'

They followed her outside where the bikes were propped up on their stands.

'Here you are.' The girl pushed two bikes towards them.

Dan was too short for his bike; he had to let the seat down. He tried to do it with the spanner the girl gave him but it kept slipping off.

'Here, let me.' The girl took the spanner from him and quickly undid the nut that fixed the seat. Then she pushed the seat down a little and turned the nut again. 'Try that,' she said.

Dan sat on the bike. 'I was just going to do that,' he lied.

'I don't think that's quite tight.' The girl gave the nut under the seat a few more turns.

'That's right, don't want to give myself an injury,' Dan laughed. The girl smiled and Pete frowned but Dan just pushed his bike off and started to ride it on the street. 'This is great!' he called. 'Wicked!'

'Can you come into the shop and pay me?' the girl asked Pete.

He followed her back into the shop where she made out the bill and gave it to him. Pete leaned against the counter, reading the bill.

'Is there anything wrong?' she asked.

Pete shook his head. 'Baggot's Bikes,' he read. 'Is that you?'

'Some of it is,' she said. 'I'm Nell Baggot. Keep the bill. It's got our phone number on. You can ring me if there's any trouble with the bikes. I'll be here all day.'

Dan had come back in while she was talking. 'I'd better keep that bill,' he said to Pete. 'You know how you're always losing things.'

'No!' Pete spoke sharply. 'I'll hold on to this.'

Dan looked shocked; Pete usually did what he told him. 'OK, let's get going!' Dan flashed a smile at Nell Baggot. 'So long, and thanks for the wheels!' He dashed back outside.

'And you owe me £5,' Pete called after him.

The girl smiled at Pete. 'Is he your brother?' she asked.

Pete shook his head. He wanted to stay and talk to her but he was too shy. He followed Dan outside. The girl stood in the shop doorway and watched as he got on to his bike.

'Bye,' she said. 'Have a good day out. You must bring the bikes back by 5 o'clock – right?'

Pete nodded. He wobbled a little as he turned to look at her. She had a smooth, tanned face and dark hair pulled back in a pony-tail and she smiled at him as she waved.

Pete stopped wobbling and smiled back at her. 'Bye... er... Nell,' he called. 'See you at 5!' He was looking forward to that, he thought.

2

A Big Mistake

Pete and Dan biked slowly along the lane out of the village. It took them a few minutes to get used to the bikes, but there was no traffic and Pete soon picked up speed and passed Dan. This was one thing that he was good at. He'd biked to school every day when he was younger and done his paper rounds on his bike. But now, his bike was clapped out and, without a job, he couldn't afford a new one. He wished he could afford one like the one he was riding now. It was magic.

'Cheers!' he called. 'See you at home next week!'

Dan pressed hard on the pedals, pushed up the gear and raced after Pete. They went on together for a mile or two until Dan began to drop back.

'Can we have a rest?' he puffed. 'And what about food? We left our sandwiches back at

Doone Hall.'

They were riding at the side of a high, stone wall which seemed to go on for ever. Pete changed gear and pushed hard on the pedals. He was going so fast that he couldn't even hear Dan puffing behind now. For the first time since they'd arrived in Devon, Pete felt happy. He'd been looking forward to the training course but felt let down. He didn't seem to be learning anything that would get him a job. And he just didn't seem to fit in with all the others. They were a noisy gang, rushing off to the pub at the end of every day, coming back singing and laughing. Pete didn't like noise, he didn't like being with a gang. He liked to do things on his own, or with Dan. Just like today, the best day of the week. Pete smiled, better slow down, he thought, give Dan a chance.

There were some big iron gates just ahead, with a long, smooth drive leading downhill all the way. Pete turned left and looked at the name on the wall at the side of the gate. 'DOONE HALL', he read as he raced past. It must be the back entrance to their hostel. Pete grinned to himself, if they pushed on they could get their sandwiches, then go off up the moors for the rest of the day.

Pete looked back; Dan was just coming round the last bend. 'Come on, Dan!' called Pete. 'Turn in here.' Pete pushed open the gate and set off up the drive.

'Wait!' called Dan. 'Where do you think you're going?'

But Pete was too far away to hear. Dan looked at the name at the side of the gate. 'DOONE HOUSE', he read. 'Oh, Pete, you stupid twit, you get everything wrong! That's not where we live.' He pushed off down the drive as fast as he could pedal.

Pete was happy. The drive was smooth and empty, his bike went well, he was moving fast. Nell must keep these bikes in good nick, he thought. I wish I had this for a week, not just for today. He heard a faint cry behind him, looked back and saw Dan waving, trying to make him wait. Pete laughed and waved back, then set off again.

Dan didn't catch up with Pete until they were at the house. Pete was sitting on the steps looking puzzled.

'What the hell do you think you're doing?' Dan puffed.

'Going a lot faster than you,' grinned Pete.

'Yes, but where to?'

'Back for some food, then we can go off all day.' For the first time Pete looked round. 'I thought this was the back of our hostel,' he said, surprised. 'The name on the gate was the same.'

'No it wasn't. This is Doone House, Pete. We're staying at Doone Hall, remember? I wish you'd be more careful!'

'You sound like my mother,' Pete grinned and stood up. 'We'd better get going then, it's uphill all the way back.'

Before Dan could reply, the door opened and a man came out. He was a big man, with a black beard and a bald head. But it wasn't the man the boys were looking at, it was his two large dogs. They were Dobermans and they stood each side of the man, looking down at the boys.

'What the hell do you think you're doing?' the man asked. 'How did you two get in here?'

'I... er... we...' said Pete, shy as ever and a bit scared too.

Dan spoke up. 'We're staying at Doone Hall and we came up your drive by mistake. We thought...'

'You thought wrong, then. This is Doone House and it's private. And those gates are kept locked. You must have got over the wall.'

'No – the gates were open – that's why...' Dan said.

'Damn and blast that driver. He should have locked them when he left.' The man glared down at the boys. 'Well, clear off back the way you came.' He scowled and his dogs moved forward.

'Hey, we only made a mistake, you know,' said Dan. 'There's no need to get stroppy with us.'

'The biggest mistake you've made is being so cheeky.' The man lifted his fist to them. 'If you don't get going right now, I'll set these dogs on you. Push off – and fast!'

The two boys got on to their bikes and set off up the drive – fast, very fast. Pete looked back and saw the man and his dogs at the bottom of the steps, waiting to see them off.

'Look out!'

Dan screamed as the blue van came round the bend too fast. The boys threw themselves on to the grass. The van tore off up to the house.

'Did you see that?' Dan was mad. He jumped up and down on the drive and made rude signs at the van. 'We might have been killed!' he shouted.

'We will be for sure if those dogs get at us,' said Pete in a shaky voice. 'Keep going!'

They kept going. Even Dan managed to go fast, round the bend and up to the gates. Then he got off his bike and stood puffing.

'I'll open them,' said Pete. 'While you get your breath back.' He went up to the gates and lifted the latch. He pushed the gate but it didn't move.

He shook the gates but they wouldn't open.

'Look!' said Dan. He pointed above Pete's head. There was a chain round the gates now. And a padlock. 'The men in that van must have locked the gate.' He looked back down the drive to the angry man and the dogs. 'What are we going to do, Pete?' he asked.

3

Dan in Trouble

Pete shook the gates until they rattled.

'Listen!' said Dan.

Pete stood still. He heard the distant barking of the dogs.

'They're coming for us!' said Dan. He was white and shaking. 'Pete, do something!'

Pete looked past the gates along the wall to where it ran past trees and bushes. 'Come on. We'd better run that way,' he said.

'What about the bikes?'

Pete had forgotten the bikes. 'Oh hell!' he said. 'We'll never get them out.' He looked round quickly. 'In here.' He threw his bike under the bushes at the side of the drive.

'But we have to take them back,' said Dan.

'We won't be taking them anywhere if those dogs get at us. Come on, hurry up!'

Pete never took the lead in anything, always left Dan to run things. But now, it seemed, he was in charge. 'Come on, Dan – this way.'

They set off along the bottom of the wall, pushing through the long grass and bushes until they came to some trees. In the distance they heard some shouting and the dogs barking again.

Dan leaned against a tree. 'They'll catch up with us soon,' he puffed.

'Not if we get over the wall.'

Dan looked up at the high stone wall. 'We'll never climb that.'

'No, but we can climb trees,' said Pete. 'Up you go!'

Dan didn't like climbing. He'd failed the rock-climbing test on the course and now Pete had to push him up into the tree. Then he led him from branch to branch until they were level with the top of the wall.

'Now,' called Pete. 'Get on that branch that leans over the wall and swing down.'

But Dan was stuck. 'I can't,' he cried. He clung to the branch and didn't move. His face was white, his eyes big with fear. 'I can't do it!'

Pete stopped. 'Yes, you can,' he said. 'I can see over the wall; there's a grassy bank, you can drop onto that, it's quite safe. Now, come on, I'll take you.'

He climbed down to Dan and pushed him gently. 'Ready?' he asked. 'Off you go!' Pete pushed hard and Dan began to slip down the branch and over the wall. Quickly Pete swung his branch right over the wall and jumped. He landed on the soft bank and turned to see Dan still clinging to his branch.

'Come on, Dan, I'll catch you,' he called. Dan screwed up his face into a silent scream and let go. He crashed into Pete and the two boys rolled down the bank onto the road. For a moment they just lay on the ground, Pete gasping, Dan groaning.

Soon, Pete sat up and dusted all the dirt off his jeans. But Dan just lay groaning in the road. 'What's wrong?' asked Pete.

'I don't know... my leg hurts... I can't move it.' Dan groaned. 'And I can't breathe.' He groaned again and shut his eyes in pain. His foot was squashed under him.

Pete sat beside him. 'Steady on, Dan, I don't think you've broken anything. Here, let me see.' Gently he lifted Dan so that he was resting against the bank. Then he gently took off his shoe.

'Ow!' cried Dan. 'That hurts.' Then he gasped for breath. 'My side hurts too,' he muttered.

Pete looked at Dan's ankle; it was puffing up fast, and turning blue. 'That's a very bad sprain,' he told his friend. 'You can't walk on that.'

'But what am I going to do?' moaned Dan. He was very pale and shaky.

'First of all you're going to rest,' said Pete. He took off his jacket and wrapped it round Dan's shoulders. For the first time, Pete was glad he'd done the training course, at least he'd learned some first aid. 'Got a hanky?' he asked Dan.

Pete took Dan's hanky and his own to a puddle at the side of the road. He dipped the hankies in the cold, dirty water and wrapped them around Dan's ankle.

'Is that any better?' he asked.

Dan nodded. His eyes were still closed but his face was a better colour.

'Come on, then,' said Pete. 'Grab my arm.'

'I just want to stay here,' said Dan. 'I feel sleepy.'

'No, you must move,' said Pete. He thought Dan might be in shock. 'Now come on – up you go!' Pete put an arm around Dan and lifted him on to his good leg. Together they hobbled down the road.

'"Here we go, here we go, here we go!"' sang Pete, trying to keep Dan's spirits up. But Dan's breathing was getting weaker and weaker.

'I must sit down,' he said. 'I can't go on right back to the village; I can hardly breathe.'

They sat at the side of the road. 'Perhaps we can hitch a lift,' said Pete.

'In that blue van, you mean?' puffed Dan.

'And end up back at Doone House,' Pete grinned. But he wasn't feeling very happy. Dan's ankle was looking awful and his breathing was bad; Pete wondered if he'd broken a rib when he fell from the tree.

'We must get on, Dan,' he said. 'Just a few more hops, eh?'

'I'll never make it to the village,' said Dan. He shifted about trying to get comfy and Pete heard something jingling in his pocket. Suddenly he knew what to do.

'Have you got a 10p piece?' he asked.

Dan fumbled in his pocket, brought out a few coins and offered them to Pete.

Pete took only the 10p piece and put it in his back pocket where he kept the bill for the bikes. 'We don't need to hop all the way to the village,' he said. 'The nearest phone box will do. We passed one on the way, it's not far from here.'

'But there's nobody at the hostel today,' moaned Dan. All the others had gone on a full day's hike across the moors and it was the warden's morning off.

'I know that, Dannyboy. I'm not going to ring the hostel,' said Pete. He patted his back pocket. 'I'm going to ring Nell,' he said.

4

Pete Gets it Right

It was hard going. The two boys staggered along the road together, Pete almost carrying Dan now.

'I can't go on, ' Dan panted. 'My ankle is hurting and even my good leg is done for.' He leaned against Pete, almost crying.

Pete held Dan up. 'It's all right,' he said. 'Take your time. We're almost at the phone box and I remember seeing a seat near it.' He lifted Dan's arm over his own shoulder and set off again.

Pete was right. They reached the phone box quite soon. Dan stretched out on the wooden seat and closed his eyes. Pete put his jacket over him again and went into the phone box. He was shaking, not only from carrying Dan; this phone call was going to be hard for Pete. He had never used a call-box before and he knew he might make a mistake.

He put the coin and the bill from the shop on the shelf and looked at the telephone. Should he put his money in or pick up the phone? Pete felt quite sick; getting away from Doone House was easy compared to this. He looked at the writing on the wall.

'Now then, look carefully – think what you're doing, Peter Walton,' he muttered to himself. Dan had only one ten-pence coin: if Pete got the number wrong they'd never get help. Step by step and very slowly, Pete read the instructions to himself, then he picked up the phone and put in his money.

'Steady on,' he told himself. This was just the point where he'd go wrong; he was always getting numbers wrong at school when he didn't check things carefully. He looked at the piece of paper. 'Right, here goes.'

He pressed each number as he said it. 4–8–9–3–2–1. There! He waited as it rang. It rang and rang, many times. Pete went cold. What was wrong? He was sure he'd got the right number. He had a sudden thought. What if there was a special code for Dimton? Damn! How could he get his money back? He looked up at the instructions again.

As he did he heard a voice at the other end of

the line.

'Dimton 489321. Baggot's Bikes, can I help you?'

Nell!

'Oh, Nell...' Pete was surprised to hear his own voice. 'Nell...'

'Hello? Can you speak up please, it must be a bad line.'

Pete took a deep breath. 'It's Pete Walton – one of the boys from the Youth Hostel...'

'Oh yes, I remember. What's happened? Are you all right?' She sounded really worried.

'Yes, er, no, er... it's Dan – you know, the other one?'

'Yes, I remember him. What's happened?' asked Nell. 'Now, just take your time and tell me where you are.'

Pete didn't know where they were. 'We're at a phone box about two miles away from a place called Doone Hall – no, I mean Doone House.'

'Doone House? That's out on the Valley Road – I know just where you mean. So what's the problem?'

'Dan's hurt his ankle – very badly. I've tried to walk him to the village but it's no use, he's quite shocked and getting weaker by the minute.'

'Put him on your bike, hide his in the hedge and

we'll collect it.'

Pete was suddenly tired; he just couldn't start telling her about the angry man and the terrible dogs and the hidden bikes.

'I can't – I'll explain later. Can you send somebody to fetch us? It's urgent. Dan's in pain and...' Pete heard his voice choke. He swallowed hard.

Nell heard his voice choke too. 'Stay there. Keep him warm. We'll be along in about ten minutes.' She put the phone down, click! Pete leaned his head against the phone box, feeling suddenly sick and faint. He shook himself, put the receiver back and stepped across to Dan who appeared to be asleep.

The next ten minutes were the longest Pete had ever known. What if Dan wasn't just asleep but ill? What if he'd given the wrong directions and Nell never found them? What if...

By the time the Land Rover pulled up beside them, Pete was shaking.

'Hi!' Nell jumped down from the passenger seat. 'How is he?' She came straight across to Dan and felt his face. 'Bring that rug, Will,' she called back to the car. 'And give us a hand.'

Pete looked up to see a man climb out of the car. He was big and strong looking, and quite young, Pete noticed.

Nell wrapped the rug around Dan. He looked up at her and smiled a sleepy, charming smile. 'Hello, darling,' he muttered.

Will picked Dan up as if he were a baby. 'Hello, darling,' he grinned. 'We'll soon have you sorted out.' And he put Dan gently down on the back seat.

Nell looked round. 'Where are the bikes?' she asked.

Pete thought quickly. He didn't want to tell the whole story in front of Will; it sounded stupid now and he was afraid they'd laugh at him.

'Er, we had to hide them,' he said. 'I just couldn't cope with the bikes and Dan.'

'So where are they?'

'Er, behind the wall, in the bushes by the entrance to Doone House.'

'*Behind* the wall? You mean you went in there?' Nell sounded worried.

Pete nodded. 'But when we came back the gates were locked so we had to climb over and...'

'And that's how your friend hurt his ankle.' Nell nodded. 'Oh, well, the bikes will probably be safe in that place. The gates haven't been open for months. And it's more important to get Dan to the surgery just now. We'll sort out the bikes later.'

'What time is it?' Pete had left his watch by the side of his bed.

'About 3 o'clock, why?'

'We have to get your bikes back by 5, don't we?'

Nell smiled, a warm, friendly smile. 'Don't worry, I won't charge you for an extra day in view of the accident.'

Pete looked at her. 'Oh, thanks,' he said gratefully.

'But it will cost you.'

Pete's heart sank. 'How much?' he asked.

'The whole story.' Nell grinned at him. 'Come on, we'll get Dan's ankle seen to, then you can tell me everything.'

They scrambled into the Land Rover. Nell squeezed between Will and Pete, Dan lay sleeping on the back seat. Now that they were safe, Pete felt very, very tired. His eyelids drooped, his head nodded, then he too, slept. On Nell's shoulder.

5

Pete Gets a Date

'So how do you feel?' Pete asked Dan.

'Shattered,' Dan grinned. He snuggled down in the narrow white bed where Nurse Stevens had put him. There was no hospital in Dimton, only a surgery with a small bedroom for emergencies. Dan was still a bit shocked, so the nurse had put him to bed until the doctor came. 'My ankle feels better now it's strapped up. Nurse says I've bruised my ribs but what I need most is a good sleep.'

Pete nodded. He'd felt much better when he woke up close to Nell. She was great. She wasn't even upset that he'd called her out, lost her bikes and then fallen asleep all over her. Pete smiled at the memory. 'I'll leave you to rest then,' he told Dan.

'And get back to the girl?' Dan grinned.

'And get back to the hostel. Ted Blackwell will

want to know where we are. Cheers! See you later.' Pete quickly left; he could do without jokes about 'the girl'. Dan was right, though: Nell was waiting for him in the surgery.

'Is he all right?' She stood up as Pete came in.

'Yeah, he's just sleepy.'

'Like you were,' smiled Nell, her dark eyes meeting his.

Pete smiled back at her. It was easy to smile at Nell, he thought, even for him.

'So, what's next?' she asked him.

'I've got to get back to Doone Hall. We've got to check in by 4 – oh, and what about the bikes?'

'You get back – I'll ring Doone House and see if I can get in. Will can run me there.'

Pete was annoyed. He wanted to get the bikes back for Nell, but now this Will bloke was taking over. 'OK.' Sadly, he turned to go. 'See you!'

'When?'

He stopped at the door. 'What do you mean?'

'When will you see me? And, if it comes to that, where? You owe me, you know... the whole story.' She stood, tall as he was, not smiling now, looking quite serious.

Pete didn't know what to say to her. He'd never had a girl ask to meet him before. 'Well, er, some of the blokes come down to the pub to play pool...' He didn't add that he never came with them; he hadn't the money to pay for drinks.

'I don't want to see any of them,' she said.

Pete blushed. 'I'm coming to see Dan after supper,' he said. 'Perhaps we could meet here?'

She nodded. 'Then you can tell me the whole story and I'll tell you about the bikes.' She looked across at him, now. 'Bye, then... for now.'

'Bye, then – see you about 7.'

Pete raced down the village street, leaping and skipping like a kid. He'd made a date with a girl! He, dim old, dull old Pete Walton was going to meet a girl. Of course there were girls back at home but he was always too shy to talk to them. They were always so busy chatting and laughing with their friends they hardly noticed him. Nell was different, she looked right at him even when Danny was there. What a girl! He tore up the drive to the hall as if he were flying. He jumped up and punched the air with his fist. What a girl! He felt full of life.

It didn't last. As soon as he saw Ted Blackwell at the door, he knew there was trouble.

'What's all this about Dan Jarvis? I had a message from the nurse at the surgery. How did all this happen?' Ted looked angry. 'I can't leave some of you people to look after yourselves for even a few hours,' he said. 'I thought I could trust you to be sensible, Pete; that's why I let you and Dan stay on your own today. So what happened?'

Pete said nothing. He felt just as if he was having yet another interview for a job he'd never get. He could never get started then, and he couldn't think where to begin now.

'I, er... well...' He looked at his feet.

'Come on, Pete. Let's have some coffee and talk about this.' Ted Blackwell led him to the warden's office and made them both a coffee. 'Right, shoot,' he told Pete, once they were sitting by the desk with their drinks.

By this time Pete had worked out what to say and the story came easily. Not all of it. Pete kept his thoughts about the Doone House people to himself. 'It was all a mistake, Ted,' he ended. 'You know what I'm like, always making mistakes. I just got us into the wrong place and then we got locked in.'

'And Dan?'

'He's fine; the nurse fixed his ankle and gave him something to kill the pain in his ribs. He was sleeping when I left.'

Ted Blackwell nodded. 'I suppose in the end, you did very well, Pete. You were very sensible. But what about the bikes?'

'Oh, Nell – er – the people from the shop are seeing to them.' Pete blushed.

Ted got up. 'Right, I'd better get down there and see what's happening to Dan.'

'I told him I'd look in later,' said Pete.

'No need, Pete, I'll sort him out now. Nurse Stevens said the doctor would be seeing him after surgery; they might even let me bring him back then.'

This was bad news. If they moved Dan, he'd have no excuse to go down to the surgery and meet Nell. 'But, Ted, I said I'd go down...'

'You just stay here; I'll see to everything.' Ted spoke firmly and Pete knew it was an order. 'You did very well, Pete. What you need now is a good supper and an early night.'

That's not what I need, thought Pete, but he didn't say anything. He just watched Ted drive the minibus down to the main road. Suddenly he felt cold and empty. Ted was right, he did need a good meal, and he was very tired. But what about Nell?

6

Nell's Secret

He'd ring her! Pete still had her number on the bill. Quickly he went upstairs and looked in his locker by his bed. He had enough change and there was a pay phone in the hall under the stairs. But where was the paper with Nell's number on? He searched his pockets. No bill, no number. He tried to think of the number he'd used that afternoon in the telephone box. It was no use. He could never remember numbers. They had no phone at home so he never had to bother. Damn, how could he get in touch with Nell if he hadn't got her number?

Suddenly Pete remembered talking to Ted in the warden's office. There was a notice-board with lots of cards and notes pinned all over it. There might be one for Baggot's Bikes. He looked up and down the hall. A few lads were sitting on the stairs waiting to use the phone but there was no sign of the warden. Pete made up his mind and stepped into the office.

Quickly he looked up and down the board, not reading, just looking for the black print with two large Bs – Baggot's Bikes. It wasn't on the top sheets; Pete flicked up the sheets and looked underneath. A police note caught his eye; it had a row of old pictures on it. 'Information wanted' ...Pete read aloud, then jumped as he heard the door open.

'Did you want something?' It was Olive, the warden. She stood at the door, looking at Pete. She was small but she still frightened him. Her name was Olive but all the boys called her Pop-eye because she was such a superman. 'The office is closed at 4,' she told Pete firmly.

'Yes, I, er, I...' Pete took a deep breath and let the notes drop. 'I was looking for information about hiring bikes,' he said. 'Somebody told me you had the number.'

Olive frowned. 'I'd have thought that you'd have given up biking,' she said, 'after what happened today.'

'Yes... well... that's just it; I want to check that everything's all right.' Pete spoke in a rush; well, it was partly true anyway.

The warden came over, flicked a few sheets

and pointed to one with Baggot's Bikes on it. 'There you are, 489321,' she said, letting the papers above fall over it. 'Right?'

It isn't right, thought Pete, I'll never remember that. 'Could I just make a note of it?' he asked and he smiled, just like Danny smiled when he wanted to charm somebody. 'And could I borrow your pen, please?' He was amazed at himself but Olive just lifted an eyebrow and handed over her pen.

Peter was glad to escape from Olive's office. He'd never had the courage to ask people like her for anything before, that was why he was in such a mess about finding a job now – he just sat still, hoping to sort things out without asking for help.

I could do with a bit of help just now, he thought, sitting on the stairs with the rest of the telephone queue and wondering why there was no one in the booth. He'd be lucky if he got Nell before she left to meet him.

'You ringing your girlfriend?' asked a young man in front. Pete jumped. How did this guy know about Nell? But the lad went on, 'There's always a rush for after 6, isn't there?'

'Is there? Why?' Pete asked.

'Cheap time for long-distance isn't it?' The guy looked at Pete as if he were daft.

But Pete smiled happily at him. Of course, that's why everyone was waiting and nobody was using the phone; they all wanted to ring home. Taking a deep breath, Pete stood up. 'Oh – I, er, I'm making a local call. All right if I go ahead?' he asked.

The rest of the gang stared at him. They weren't used to Pete Walton asking anything. 'Yeah – go ahead,' said one. 'You ringing Dan Jarvis? I heard he had an accident.'

'Yeah, he's all right now, thanks.' Pete went to the phone and called Nell's number.

'Nell? Look, I can't get down to the village. Ted, our leader, says I've got to rest tonight.'

'Oh, Pete, no! I must see you – something very odd's happened.' For once, Nell sounded really worried.

'Is it about the bikes?'

'Yes. That man at Doone House said he'd seen you go off up the drive. He says you must have pinched them!'

'If that was the man we met at the door I'm not surprised. He was a right villain. There's something odd about that set-up. I was going to tell you all about it tonight...'

'What if I came up there?'

Pete was horrified. 'You can't do that,' he said. 'Everyone would see you.'

'So? You ashamed of me or something?'

'Oh, no.' Pete was ashamed of himself now for upsetting her. 'No, it's not that, it's just... I wouldn't know where to meet you.'

'Stables – 9 o'clock. I know a back way. Nobody will see me.'

Pete hesitated. Was there no stopping this girl? Then he smiled into the phone. He didn't want to stop her anyway.

Somebody prodded his back, hard. 'Hey, mate, you saying sweet nothings in Dannyboy's ear? Come on, it's nearly time.' A lad from the front of the queue spoke. 'Get a move on!'

'OK – er – right – see you, then.' He daren't use her name, not with that gang behind him. He put the phone down and backed out.

'All yours,' he said, and went off in search of supper.

But he couldn't enjoy his food. He was very hungry but too much on edge to eat. He had a bowl of soup and some bread, then left the dining-room to flop in front of the TV.

He was fast asleep when Dan came back. One of the boys thumped his shoulder and woke him to tell him. For a moment, Pete didn't remember where he was. He shook his head and blinked, then he remembered. Hell, what time was it? He rushed out to the hall to look at the old clock but he was in too much of a hurry to see properly. Was it 20 to 9, or a quarter to 8? He ran off upstairs to see Dan.

'You coming to bed, then?' Dan asked, cheerfully now. He was propped up in bed with a tray of supper, eating happily. Pete looked at the food and felt sick.

'Er... no... not yet. What's the time?'

'Honestly, Pete, you just passed the clock in the hall.'

'Yeah, I know, but I passed it too quick. I was in such a hurry to see you, Dannyboy.'

Dan laughed. 'It's nearly quarter to 9,' he said. 'Time for beddy-byes. Olive's coming to tuck me up soon.'

'Well, ...I need a bit of fresh air. I'll just have a stroll outside – be in later, all right?'

'Haven't you had enough fresh air today?' said Dan, tucking into his pudding. 'Don't mind me – go ahead!'

Pete went downstairs. A crowd of boys was getting ready to go down to play pool so nobody noticed him leaving. As the rest of them set off for the village, Pete walked round the back of the house and across to the stables.

He sat there, in the dark waiting for Nell. It was

so quiet he could hear the church clock, down in the village, striking 9. He sat a few minutes longer, but still she didn't come. What had happened to her? What if Ted had seen her, or worse Popeye? What if her parents wouldn't let her out? What if she was with that bloke, Will? Pete stood up and walked around. It seemed like hours since the clock had struck. Where was she?

7

The Plan

'Boo!'

Pete jumped and looked round

'You were asleep,' said Nell. 'I caught you napping!'

'You got here!' said Pete.

She smiled at him. 'I got here,' she said. 'At last.'

'Well...' said Pete. He just stood there, looking at Nell.

'Well,' said Nell. 'So what happened up at Doone House? Tell me all about it.'

They sat on an old bench and Pete told her about the man and his terrible dogs at Doone House.

'I'm surprised you even got in there,' said Nell. 'Those gates have been locked all summer, ever since Lady Bartram died. I heard that her cousin Mary was coming from America to take over

Doone House but she's not been seen. Perhaps this man is some sort of an agent?'

'So why was he so hard on us? We only made a mistake.'

'Perhaps he thought you were vandals or something.'

Pete laughed. 'Did we look like vandals?' Then he had an idea. 'I suppose he could have been a guard. Is there anything valuable in Doone House?'

'Oh yes,' Nell said. 'It's a beautiful place, full of antiques and valuable paintings. I know it well because my mum used to work up there, cleaning and polishing the lovely furniture. She used to take my sister and me with her, when we were kids.'

As she spoke, Pete remembered the blue van that had almost run them over. He had a funny feeling he was on to something but before he could think what it was, he remembered the bikes.

'Hey, listen, if that bloke says we've got the bikes, it means he doesn't know where they are. Right?'

Nell nodded. 'Unless he's kept them for some reason.'

'I don't think he'd do that. After all, you'd report it to the police and he doesn't seem to want anybody looking round there.'

'So who's got the bikes, then?'

'Nobody. He thinks we biked away so he hasn't found them yet.'

Pete thought for a moment. 'I can remember where we hid them so I'll go back and get them tomorrow. No sweat.' He sat back on the bench, feeling really good.

'But you can't, Pete!' Nell sounded quite alarmed. 'You said yourself that man was tough and the dogs were dangerous. How will you get in? And even more important, how will you get out?'

Pete got up and walked across to the barn wall where ropes and climbing tools hung. 'See this?' He held up a rope ladder with hooks at the end and some thin, nylon rope. 'Just hook that on to the wall – I'll be over in no time. I learned how to do that just the other day.'

'But you'll never get the bikes over the wall on your own.'

'Well, I could. It would be quicker with two but Dan's no use, now.' Pete was silent. He didn't want to admit that he had no other friends. On the other hand, he didn't want that Will's help. Getting the bikes back for Nell had suddenly become the most important thing he had ever done and he wanted to do it himself.

'I'll go with you.' Nell spoke softly.

'You?' Pete thought how good it would be to have Nell at his side while he performed the great deed. 'But it might be dangerous,' he said.

'No more dangerous for me than for you – less, perhaps. I know the house and grounds. I played there every holiday while Mum did the cleaning.'

Before Pete could protest there was a loud bang from the barn next door. They heard footsteps moving towards the stable.

'Somebody coming,' whispered Nell.

'Coming to lock up,' said Pete. 'Quick – we'll have to get out this end.'

He grabbed Nell's hand and led her outside. They pressed themselves into the shadows of the stables as the caretaker passed in through the door. They stood rigid while he locked up and went back to the kitchens. Pete let out a great sigh – but he didn't let go of Nell's hand.

'I'll have to go in,' he said. 'They'll be locking the front door soon.'

'What time tomorrow?'

'I don't know – I'm in the rock-climbing set; I'll have to get out of it. I'll be doing plenty of climbing anyway.' He grinned.

Nell grinned back. 'I'll be at the shop, ready to go at any time.' She waited. 'See yah!' she said.

'Mmmm,' he whispered. He could smell the

shampoo on her hair, the soap on her skin. Suddenly he put his arms around her and pulled her to him. Then he kissed her. And, better still, she pressed right up against him and kissed him back, hard.

❖

'Where've you been?' asked Dan. 'There's been all hell on up here, first Popeye hunting for you, then Ted asking questions...'

Pete didn't answer. Pete couldn't answer; in his mind, he was still standing in the shadow of the barn, kissing Nell.

'Pete! What've you been doing?' Dan sounded well awake now and not very pleased.

'What – I – er – I –' Pete, on the other hand, seemed half asleep.

'Aw, you're worse than usual. Take a deep breath and start again.'

Pete did so, very slowly, so that he had time to think of his story. 'I was in the stables,' he told Dan. 'Sorting out some climbing stuff for tomorrow.' Well, that was true anyway.

Dan was surprised. Pete never thought about tomorrow; he was always forgetting to see people about a job or to post his applications. Once, he'd even forgotten to sign on! But now, he was all prepared for tomorrow's climb.

'You're in the climbing group tomorrow?' Dan asked.

Pete remembered that Dan wouldn't be able to climb; he wouldn't even be able to walk much. But he might be very useful. 'Would you like me to stay with you?' he asked.

'Nah – you'll want to go climbing.'

'Yes, I do, but not with Ted and his gang...'

Pete explained about the bikes and his plan to get them out. 'So if we can get a lift down to the village, you could look after the shop for Nell while we get the bikes, couldn't you?'

Dan looked pleased. 'Hey – that's a great idea, Pete!' he said, surprised that Pete had thought of it. 'I've always wanted to work in a shop,' he went on. 'And Popeye has lent me some crutches so I can get out a bit.'

'I'll go and tell them I'm back and fix it all up,' said Pete. 'Then we'd better get some sleep. Tomorrow's going to be a busy day.'

8

Dan Looks After the Shop

❖

The boys weren't at all busy the next morning; they slept in. It was 10 o'clock before Popeye woke them up.

'Come on, you two,' she said. 'You missed breakfast long ago.'

Pete sat up. 'What time is it?' he asked.

'Almost 10 – and Nurse Stevens is waiting to look at Dan's ankle. You'd better get moving.' She stomped off downstairs.

Dan groaned and snuggled back into his sleeping-bag. Pete jumped up, had a quick wash down and cleaned his teeth as he talked to Dan.

'How are we going to get down to the village? The minibus will have gone long ago. I hope Popeye will give us a lift.' There was no reply. Dan was asleep again. Pete took his sponge over to Dan's bed. 'Here, let me help you,' he said. He squeezed cold water on to Dan's face.

'Ahhh!' Dan shot up. 'You rotten swine!'

'It worked, though, didn't it?' Pete grinned. 'Now let me help you over to the wash-basin.' Pete felt so happy he could have danced across the bedroom but Dan wasn't doing any dancing. He hopped around while Pete got him dressed.

Nurse Stevens was waiting in the kitchen, drinking coffee with Popeye. While Dan had his ankle dressed, Pete made them both some tea and toast.

'You going down to the village?' he asked Popeye.

She shook her head. 'I'm working here all day,' she said.

Damn! How could he get Dan to the shop?

'There you are, laddie,' said Nurse Stevens. 'That's going on very nicely now.' She packed her bag. 'I must rush off, Olive, it's my baby day.'

'And Dan's been the first, has he?' laughed Olive.

Dan scowled, but suddenly Pete knew what to do. 'Can you give Dan and me a lift to Dimton?' he asked Nurse Stevens.

'Aye, if you're ready right now,' she said.

'Give us five minutes,' Pete promised. He rushed round getting Dan's coat, his crutches, his money, and – most important – the rope and the ladder, which he hid under his jacket.

'Where are you going to?' Nurse Stevens asked them as she dropped them off in Dimton.

'Oh, Dan's got a thing going with that girl at the bike shop,' said Pete. 'He just wants to go and see her.' He grinned at Dan's surprise.

For once Dan blushed. 'It's not me...' he started, but Pete took him by the arm and almost dragged him into the shop.

The bell on the door pinged and Will came out from the back. This was a blow, Pete had expected Nell.

'Oh, hi! You feeling better?' Will asked Dan.

'Yeah, can't do much walking, though.'

'Or biking,' said Will. 'So what are you doing here?'

Suddenly Pete dried up. He didn't know what to tell Will.

As usual, Dan did. 'I've come to help,' he said. 'It's boring up at the hall with everybody away climbing.'

'Right; that's handy for Nell,' said Will. 'She has to go out this afternoon.'

She did? Pete felt a bit sick. Most of the morning was gone anyway, there was no sign of Nell and they hadn't even set off to rescue the bikes yet.

'Where is she now?' he asked.

'At the bank. It's open on Wednesdays,' said Will. 'I'm just looking after the shop until she gets back.'

'We can do that,' said Pete. 'I'm good with bikes...'

'Except when you lose them,' grinned Will.

Pete wanted to hit him. 'I'll get them back,' he said, coldly.

'Oh, yes,' said Will. 'You and who else?' He looked at Dan's crutches.

Just then, Nell came in. She looked very smart in black jeans and jacket, with a red scarf around her neck. Pete just stood and looked at her.

'Hi!' Dan said. 'You're looking very smart.'

'Oh, thank goodness you two have arrived,' she said. 'I've just been at the bank having a terrible time.' She turned to Will. 'Tell Mum that we've both got to see the bank manager next week. You know what that means, don't you?'

Will nodded. 'No more Baggot's Bikes. If you can just get him to hang on until the summer holidays I know you'll be all right.'

'I know that, you know that, but he won't wait.' Nell looked gloomy.

'Look, I've got to go,' said Will. 'Nurse Stevens is coming to see the baby this morning and I promised to look in.'

'Of course – love to Jenny and Mum – and a kiss to little William from me; 'bye, Will.' She saw him out and shut the door.

Pete was thinking hard. 'So that Will – he's...?'

'My sister's husband,' said Nell. She smiled at him as if she knew what he'd been thinking. 'He's good to me and Mum. He puts in hours at the bikes when he's finished working at the garage, so Mum's up there helping with the new baby. We couldn't have kept the shop going without Will after Dad died.' She sighed. 'If only the bank manager will give me a bit longer, I'm sure I can make it pay.'

'Just leave me in charge – I'll bring the customers in,' said Dan. He put on his most winning smile. 'There – they'll never resist me!'

Nell smiled at Dan and showed him round so that he could sell things or hire bikes to the customers who came in. Pete smiled, too. He felt very happy now that he knew how Will fitted into the picture. Soon, Dan was settled behind the counter with his crutches and a flask of coffee and sandwiches which Nell had made for him.

'Off you go, you two love-birds,' said Dan, waving them off. 'I'll be in charge here – ring me if they set the dogs on you!'

Nell and Pete set off across the fields. 'Do you think they will?' asked Nell. She had changed into blue jeans, and tied her hair up with the red scarf.

'What?' Pete had been looking at her, not listening.

'Set the dogs on us?'

Pete shook his head. 'They'll never know we're there,' he said.

'We won't go near the drive or the house.'

They walked on, Nell striding out in step with Pete. She slipped her hand through his arm. He squeezed it tight. 'Love-birds', Dan had called them. Pete looked across at Nell and smiled. Well, birds could fly, couldn't they? Even over walls? He felt everything was going to be all right.

9

Locked In

It was easy getting in. Pete slung the hooks on the rope ladder over the top of the wall, then he climbed up, sat on the wall, and turned the ladder round so that he could clamber down the other side. Nell waited outside to get the bikes as he pulled them up on the nylon rope and lowered them down to her.

'Dead simple,' said Pete.

And the first part was. Pete was thin but strong. He climbed over the wall easily. The trouble started on the other side. Pete dropped off the ladder and looked round the long grass and the bushes where the bikes were hidden. He found the right bushes, but no bikes.

'Oh, hell, they've gone!' he cursed.

Nell looked through the gates. 'But how?' she asked. 'Even if somebody found them how could they get them over the wall?'

They stood looking at each other through the bars of the gate. Pete said, 'I think somebody must have found them.'

'It could have been the men who were chasing you and Dan,' said Nell.

'Yes – and they've taken the bikes away.'

'But why?'

Pete shook his head. 'I don't know. Maybe to make trouble for Dan and me – or for you?'

Nell looked worried. 'It will make trouble for me if I lose two of my best bikes,' she said. 'There's hundreds of pounds there.' Nell looked very worried and her eyes filled with tears.

Pete looked at her through the bars of the gate. 'Don't cry,' he said. 'Please, don't cry, Nell.' He pushed his arms through the bars and held her.

Nell sniffed and shook her dark head. Then Pete had an idea. 'Is there a garage or a stable up at the house?' he asked.

Nell nodded. 'There's a big garage where Lady Bartram's car was kept.'

'I'll bet that's where they've taken the bikes,' said Pete. 'They'd never take bikes into Doone House. Now, don't you worry, I'll go and look for them.'

'And I'll come with you.' Nell smiled and

gripped his hands. 'I know the place better than you do. And if you do find the bikes it'll take two of us to ride them back here.'

Pete thought he should say no, but he wanted to be with Nell. 'OK,' he said. 'You win.' He climbed up to the top of the wall and threw the ladder down for Nell. She climbed up quickly and easily, then they moved the ladder and both climbed down the other side.

'I'll show you the way,' she said when they landed. 'I know every little path through this park; I loved this place when I was a kid. Come on!'

Nell led the way through the trees, down the hill and round the back of the house. She took Pete to a long building with huge double doors which were locked with a chain and a very new padlock.

Pete groaned. 'If they are in there,' he said, 'we'll never get them.'

But Nell smiled. 'There's another door at the side,' she told him. 'Let's try it.'

They crept round the side of the barn to a small, black door. Nell rattled the handle and it opened. She stepped inside. 'Come in,' she said, holding the door open for Pete as if he were a visitor. 'Welcome to my childhood playground!'

Pete passed through the doorway. Nell closed

the door after him and they looked round. It was very dark in the barn, the windows were broken and thick with cobwebs.

'Spooky,' whispered Pete. As soon as his eyes got used to the darkness he could see that the place was stacked full of things. Huge shapes, some of them covered in white sheets, loomed out of the shadows. Pete shivered. 'There wasn't much room for a kid to play in here.'

But Nell shook her head. 'There used to be,' she said. 'It was always empty except for the car.' She looked all round. 'Hey, some of this stuff is from Doone House. We used to help Mum polish it. Look!' She rubbed her hand on a small oval table. 'That was in Lady Bartram's bedroom.'

'Perhaps that new man doesn't like antiques.'

'Well, he wouldn't just leave them out here. He'd sell them.'

'He might be going to have a sale.'

Nell shook her head. 'Not like this,' she said. 'They'd have it all on show up at the house – a proper sale. We're talking mega-bucks here, Pete, not junk. There's something funny going on...'

Pete laughed. 'Here's something that looks funny,' he said. 'Look at this!' He pulled an old sheet off a huge four-poster bed. There, on the bare mattress, lay the two bikes, side by side as if sleeping. 'I've found them,' said Pete. 'Quick, grab one, I'll get the other and we'll get out of here before anyone sees us.'

'Shhh!' Nell held up her hand. Pete heard the sound of a voice outside, a voice he knew. It was the man with the dogs. Pete closed his eyes. If the dogs were with him they'd soon get their scent. But the man just went on muttering to himself.

'...those fools never remember to lock up.' Then, click, somebody locked the side door!

They waited until the voice died away, then Pete let out a groan. 'I don't believe this,' he said. 'First Dan and I get locked in, then we get out and the bikes are locked in and now you and I have got locked in with the bikes! It's like one of those computer games.'

'Only it's real,' said Nell. She moved amongst the furniture until she found a tall, carved chair. 'Look at this,' she said, sitting in it. 'This stood in the hall near the front door. It's got little animals carved on the arms and legs. Mum said it was hundreds of years old, made for a prince.'

'Suits a princess, just as well,' said Pete, amazing himself.

'Thanks, Pete,' Nell said. Then she frowned. 'But there's something funny about all this, you know. I'm worried.'

'So am I,' he agreed. 'If that man comes back with his dogs we're done for.'

'No, I mean about all this stuff. It's not all from Doone House; he must have collected it from all over the place. I can't help feeling...' But before Nell could go on, there was a noise at the big double doors.

'Shhh – come here,' said Pete. He grabbed Nell's hand and pulled her under the huge bed. 'I hope nobody wants to buy this today,' he whispered in Nell's ear.

'I hope nobody wants to buy it ever,' she whispered back. 'It belongs in the green bedroom at Doone House.'

Pete could tell she was upset at the idea of Doone House losing its furniture so he put an arm round her. He felt warm and happy, even with danger so near. He wanted to stay hidden with Nell for ever. She snuggled close to him and they lay still, listening to the big doors opening and the sound of an engine as a car was driven into the barn.

10

Quick Thinking

I bet that's the blue van, thought Pete. He tried to turn his head to see if he was right but it was no use, the van was only a dark shape in the doorway.

'Got the list?' said a man's voice.

'Yeah – we've got to take them big pictures up to Overton Mill.' This sounded like a younger man.

'Right – I'll take them bikes I found as well,' the older man said. 'I can drop them at my mate's on the way. Worth a few quid, they are.'

'I'll be glad to see the back of them. What if those lads go to the police?'

'Let 'em. By the time my mate's done with 'em, nobody'll be able to identify 'em.'

'If the boss knew you were doing a bit of business on the side he'd do his nut.'

'And if his sister knew he was stripping her house

she'd do it for him!' The older man laughed at his joke.

'Her and a few others. The cops have got a list of pictures from all the houses he's done.' The younger man sounded worried. 'I only hope they're not after us.'

'Oh, don't panic, young Gary. The boss really is a Bartram; the cops were very impressed when they came to check up. "Cleaning and restoring" he told 'em.' The man laughed again. 'Cleaning his sister out, more like. Well, let's get on then. Give us a hand with these pictures.'

Nell and Pete lay very still. From under the bed, they heard the men grunting and panting as they loaded the van.

'They're taking Lady Bartram's pictures!' Nell muttered. 'Some are worth a fortune!'

'Shhh,' said Pete. He was trying to think of a plan to get them out and it wasn't easy with Nell in his arms. But then he heard something that made him forget even Nell for a moment.

'Hang about,' the younger man said. 'We'll have to get 'em signed for and the boss hasn't given us the papers. There'll be all hell on if we forget anything this time. That's how those lads on the bikes got in yesterday – you forgetting to lock the gates.'

'Not only me, mate. I'm just the driver. You're in charge of them gates.'

'How the hell can I stay to lock the gates when you're all set to do 90 down the drive?'

The driver laughed. 'Next time I'll pull up for you, all right?'

'Yeah, well, make sure you do. I'll get over to the house now,' said Gary. He moved towards the side door. 'You can lock up here and bring the van round the front.'

Pete's heart sank; they'd never get away if the driver locked all the garage doors. He was just thinking they should make a dash for it when a huge pair of Doc Marten's stopped by the side of the bed.

'We'll have to rent a truck when he sells that,' said Gary.

A pair of shabby sneakers joined the Doc Martens. Pete and Nell were shaking so much they felt sure the men would hear them. 'Who the hell would buy a thing like that?' said the older man.

'Boss must know somebody as wants it, else it wouldn't be out here. He only shifts stuff he knows he can sell,' Gary said.

'Nice bit of overtime when we move that,' laughed the other man.

'I'll go and get them papers,' said Gary. The

Doc Marten's turned and moved away. 'You load them blasted bikes and meet me at the front. Right? And for God's sake don't forget to lock up.'

The sneakers plodded past the bed now, on their way to the side door. There was the rattle of keys, the door was opened, slammed shut, and locked. The one pair of feet came back towards the bed. Towards the bikes.

'Now!' said Pete. 'Let's get him!' He just hoped Nell knew what he was going to do. There'd been no chance to tell her.

They slid out from under the bed, pulling the man's legs from under him. Pete threw himself on top of him. He sat on the man's chest and tied his legs together with the nylon rope he'd brought for lifting the bikes over the wall. Nell took the man's head and gagged him with her red scarf. The man seemed dazed by his fall. He didn't put up much of a struggle. Pete was glad; he didn't want to hurt him. Nell did, though; she tied the gag so hard that Pete thought she would choke him.

Grabbing the bikes off the bed, they ran past the van through the big doors and outside.

'Let's go!' Pete shouted.

It was hard work, biking up the hill, through the trees and over the grass, but they had good mountain bikes and they were both strong bikers.

There wasn't much time, Pete knew. As soon as Gary came out and found the van wasn't at the front he'd go back to the garage and find his mate tied up.

'Keep going, we're nearly there now,' puffed Pete.

But even as he spoke, they heard people shouting and the deep barking of the dogs. The voices sounded far away but the barking was coming closer.

'They've let the dogs out!' cried Nell. She was racing along, her hair streaming loose behind her. Even with all the danger, Pete had time to think how marvellous she looked.

But he knew that if the dogs picked up their trail they were really in trouble. 'Keep going – faster!' he called to Nell. 'You go over on the ladder. I'll climb a tree – we'll have to leave the bikes again.'

Nell pushed on; she was quicker than Pete. Suddenly he saw her pointing ahead and shouting to him. She raced her bike through the trees, past their ladder, right on to the drive.

What's she doing? thought Pete. If they see her there we'll never get away. He saw Nell riding up the drive, up to the gates – and right between them! Then she stopped and waved Pete on.

'These two clowns will be in trouble,' she

grinned. 'I saw the chain hanging lose and guessed they'd left it unlocked.'

Quickly, Pete pulled a short bit of chain to the outside of the gates and snapped the lock. All the men were locked inside the grounds of Doone House now.

'That'll take a bit of sorting out,' he said. 'Oh, Nell, I'm glad you're safe!'

She smiled across at him. 'I'm glad we both are – and we've got the bikes.'

'So let's get down to the police station then.' Pete started off.

'There isn't one.' Nell pedalled alongside.

'What?'

'A police station – we don't have one in Dimton. Nearest one is ten miles away. We'll have to ring from the shop.'

They biked on. It was easy now that they were on the road, but it was as much as he could do to keep up with Nell. She was a very fast biker. Pete puffed after her. He was glad they'd got away but he was worried about what to do next. What if the police wouldn't listen to them? What if Nell left all the talking to him? He knew he'd get in a mess but he didn't want to ask her to do it. He pushed on behind Nell, feeling very gloomy.

'Hi, love-birds,' said Dan as they rushed into the

shop. They looked at each other and grinned. They were out of breath and couldn't even speak for a moment. Nell's dark hair hung over her pink face. Pete was sweating right through his shirt. They just stood, hand in hand, leaning on the counter.

'You got the bikes, then,' said Dan.

'Here,' panted Nell. She took a card from a rack above Dan's head and pushed it over to him. 'Ring this number.'

Dan looked at the card. 'Police?' he asked. 'But you've got the bikes back.'

'Do it,' said Nell. She stood breathing heavily and watched Dan. When he got through she took the phone from him. Pete was glad she was going to talk to the police, but he was surprised at what she said.

'Tracy? It's Nell. Is Rick out on the cars? Right, send him to Doone House – yes, now! And send a few more men as well – there might be trouble. We've seen some men shifting a lot of pictures – they're taking them to Overton Mill – you might need somebody out there, too. Yes – I'm sure – believe me, Tracy. Just get the cars there – all right?' Nell put the phone down and pushed back her hair.

Dan looked at her and whistled. 'You really get

things buzzing, don't you? What's it all about, then?'

Nell smiled. 'My sister was at school with Tracy,' she said. 'She'll believe me. Now, give us a cup of your coffee, Dan, and we'll tell you all about it.'

So Pete and Nell sat on the counter and told Dan all that had happened. Dan was really fed up to have missed all the fun.

'You mean Pete nobbled the man and tied him up?' he asked Nell.

'It was the only thing I could do,' said Pete, smiling. 'I don't think I hurt him much.'

'I could have choked him,' said Nell, looking angry. 'When I think of how my mum looked after those beautiful things, all the years of dusting and polishing...' She was nearly crying with rage.

Dan gave her another cup of coffee. Pete gave her a hug.

'Calm down, Nell,' he said. 'It'll be all right now you've sent in the heavies!'

'If it is all right, it's thanks to you,' said Nell. 'Oh, Pete, you were terrific!' And she threw her arms around him and kissed him, hard.

Pete was so surprised he forgot to feel shy and kissed her back. Dan clapped his hands and cheered!

11

A Hero at Last

❖

Pete sat on the shop floor, fitting a wheel on a bike. They were all still waiting for news from Doone House.

'It's lovely and quiet in here,' he said.

'That's the trouble,' said Nell. 'I need a lot more customers or the bank manager will make me close the shop.'

'Is it your shop?' Dan asked her.

'Sort of,' she said. 'It's a family business but Mum's not interested in bikes and I'm mad about them so I took over when Dad died. Mum does all the bookings when we're busy – if we keep open till then.' She looked worried. 'If only I can pay something in this week, that'll keep the bank off my back. I know we'll be all right when the summer holidays start.'

'Hey, I've got a great idea!' said Dan. 'What if

we get our lot to take bikes out for a day?' he said. 'We have another free day on Friday.'

'If you could do that,' said Nell, 'the money would be in the bank next week.' She smiled at Dan and then across at Pete. 'I'm sure we'll do well in the summer holidays.'

'What you need is publicity,' said Dan. 'I'll do some leaflets for you. My dad's a printer; he'll let me do them cheap.'

Pete nodded happily. He was enjoying working in the quiet shop with bikes he loved. He wanted to stay and work there all day, every day, but he knew he couldn't. Nell couldn't afford to give anyone a job and, anyway, he lived miles away.

'We'll have to get back to the hostel before Ted's lot,' he said, standing up and turning the mended bike over, 'or we'll be in trouble again. I'll just go and wash my hands.'

Pete was in the wash-room when he heard the doorbell ring, then voices in the shop. Perhaps Nell had got a customer at last. But when he went back into the shop he saw it was a policeman and policewoman.

'This is Tracy and Rick. Well, Sergeant Downs and PC Webley, now,' Nell told him. 'We've got to make statements, Pete.'

'You first, I think,' said the policewoman to Dan.

'OK, PC Webley,' said Dan, smiling his best smile at the policewoman. 'Where's your notebook?'

The policewoman smiled. 'I'm Sergeant Downs,' she said. 'PC Webley will take your statement, won't you, Rick?'

PC Webley took out his notebook and pen. 'Off you go,' he said.

Dan told them what had happened the day before. '...so we had to get the bikes back,' he finished. 'That's what Nell and Pete were doing today.'

Nell then told her part of the story. As she told it, Pete was amazed to hear how much he'd done. 'Then Pete said..., then Pete did...' By the time she had finished he was blushing – again!

'So, you're the hero,' said Sergeant Downs. 'We thought there was something odd going on up at Doone House, but that man with the dogs really is old Lady Bartram's cousin. He told us that he was just guarding the house and getting things ready for his sister, Lady Mary, so there was nothing we could do.' She smiled at Pete. 'And we were so busy working on the local art robberies that we couldn't keep watch on Doone House day and night. Now you've solved both problems, tell us how you did it.'

The policeman flipped over a new page in his notebook and smiled at Pete, just like the people who interviewed him for jobs did. And Pete felt just like he did when he was having an interview, speechless and hopeless.

'Er... er...' he said. He swallowed hard and looked round the room as if to escape. But his eyes met Nell's. She smiled and nodded to him. 'Go on, Pete,' she whispered. 'You can do it.'

And he did. Suddenly, Pete found that he could say everything, clearly and easily, without muttering or stumbling. He told the police how it had all happened, from the moment he and Dan took the wrong turning, right up to the time of the call to the police station. Then he sat back and beamed at Nell. She smiled at him proudly and turned to Sergeant Downs.

'Have you saved the Doone House pictures, Tracy?' asked Nell.

'Did you get the crooks?' asked Pete.

'Can you give us a lift back to the hostel?' asked Dan.

The sergeant laughed. 'Yes, on all three counts,' she said. 'And thank you all very much. If you ever want a job with the police, just come to me for a reference.'

❖

When Dan and Pete arrived back at Doone Hall in a police car, Ted Blackwell looked shocked. But when he heard what Pete had done his expression changed.

'I always thought there was more to you than we ever saw, Pete,' he said. 'You've got your wits about you, well done!'

After supper he packed them all into the minibus and drove them down to the village pub. Even Popeye took time off to come with them. Pete fetched Nell over from the shop but he didn't have time to talk to her. People kept coming to congratulate him on saving the Doone House treasures. At first, Pete felt shy; he just smiled and mumbled, looking all round for Dan to come and help him out. But Dan was busy chatting up a group of girls at the other end of the room and Nell was busy talking to Ted Blackwell. It was Will who came over and helped him out. He slapped Pete on the back and introduced people to him. Pete found that he liked Will now, and what's more, he liked being part of the crowd in the pub. He looked over to Nell, who was listening to something Ted was saying.

Ted Blackwell was booking bikes for Friday. He

even gave Nell a cheque so that she could post it to the bank the next day.

'Thank you,' said Nell. 'You don't know how much I need this.' As she took the cheque she met Pete's gaze and smiled right at him. Pete glowed and moved over to her side.

'Oh, I think your problems may be over,' Pop-eye told Nell. 'Did you know there's a reward for finding the pictures? Of course, you'll have to share it with the boys...' She smiled over at Pete and across the room to Dan. 'But I've heard that Lady Mary is planning to open Doone House to the public next year. She's very keen on the tourist trade. She'll be interested in your cycle-hire business, I'm sure.'

'So am I,' whispered Pete to Nell. 'You can take my share of the reward so long as I can come to work for you in the summer holidays. With Dan's leaflets and my work on the bikes, you'll be able to take cycle tours out to Doone House.'

Nell smiled happily at him.

At closing time, the boys all piled back into the minibus – except for Pete. 'Goodnight,' he said. 'Shall I see you tomorrow?'

'What about the rock-climbing?'

Pete smiled. 'I'll stay and keep Dan company. We can go on mending the bikes ready for your great rush on Friday.'

Nell smiled at him. 'Thanks, Pete,' she said. 'You're great.'

Pete bent quickly over and kissed her. All the boys were looking out of the minibus windows.

'Whoooo!' they shouted. Ted Blackwell revved the engine.

''Night, Nell. See yah!' Pete called from the step. He slid the door shut and sank down on the front seat next to Dan.

'What's best,' asked Dan. 'Being a love-bird or a hero?'

Pete grinned. 'Best to be both,' he said. He looked out of the window at Nell standing by her shop. 'Tell you what, when we get back home I'm going to join that business course Ted told us about.'

'Why?' asked Dan. 'You never wanted to before.'

'I never wanted to run a business before,' smiled Pete. He waved to Nell as the minibus took them along the village street, past the little bike shop on the corner.